What Those Light Years Carry

What Those Light Years Carry

Poems by

Aden Thomas

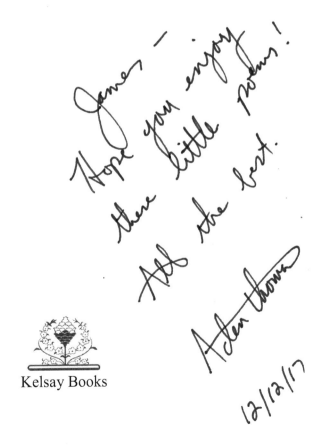

Kelsay Books

Cover: Cynthia Chase-Gray, *Clouds* 2016

ISBN: 13-978-1-945752-97-1

Kelsay Books
Aldrich Press
www.kelsaybooks.com

For Christine Watne, Cynthia Chace-Gray,
and Patricia Frolander—
all who said I could...

Acknowledgments

I want to express my deepest appreciation to the following individuals and organization who have supported my writing and have kept me going (even in a small way) over the years: my family, Cynthia Chace-Gray, Ron Chesmore, William Missouri Downs, Mark Ducker, Dr. Susan Frye, Patricia Frolander, Justin Garrity, Dagoberto Gilb, Rebecca Hilliker, Christina Kuzmych, Clifford Marks, Mathew Rottweiler, Shannon Smith, Alarie Tennille, Christine Watne, The Wyoming Humanities Council, WyoPoets, Wyoming Writer's Inc., and Wyoming Public Media.

Many of these poems in this volume first appeared, sometimes in slightly different forms, in the following publications:

The Kentucky Review, Absinthe Poetry Review, Glass: Facets of Poetry, Dressing Room Poetry Journal, The Magnolia Review, VAYAVYA, Poetry Quarterly, The Inflectionist Review, Gyroscope Review, The Avalon Literary Review, The Red River Review, San Pedro Review, MockingHeart Review, Jawline, The Eunoia Review, SEVERINE, Ibis Head Review, Shot Glass Journal, The Lake, Common Ground Review, Third Wednesday, Burning Wood Literary Journal, The Milo Review, Nixes Mate, Up The Staircase Quarterly, Turtle Island, Autumn Sky, The Road Not Taken, Scarlett Leaf Review, Muddy River Poetry Review, Rising Phoenix Review, Ink in Thirds, Halcyon Days, Skylark Review, The Virginia Normal, The Big Windows Review and *The Yellow Chair Review.*

Contents

Preface to My Poetry

You want to watch the sky
for weather patterns,
the way the clouds shapeshift
into things you've never seen.

You want to feel the path, the journey through.
Listen to the words, their beating wings,
fly to you from the treetops of meaning.
Trace their feathers to the sounds.

Let migration find always the possibility
of rain. Run to the forest.
The fog has settled there
with the great white owl from across the sea.

The Calling

Snowflakes fall against the window.
You touch cold glass.
This time something is there on the other side,
a voice you feel but cannot understand, a whisper.

The wind outside carves your reflection
in crystal flurries hanging from the moon.
You run your fingers across the glass, trace
the contours of your mouth and eyes and cheeks.

The next morning, only crows face the cold.
You walk into the forest without your shoes or coat,
listening to their caws.
You yell back, whatever comes rushing from your chest,
words you think you might have known before.

Your calls echo across the snow.

Winter's Autumn

All these silver leaves
pinched from their cloudy branches
now cascade and twist
down to the earth in flurries.

If only you came so easily
from such distances,
shaken from the sky,
spinning down to me.

I would stand outside all night
without my gloves or coat,
catching your riches
on my outstretched and wooden arms.

Mistress Wind

She dances through a dragon's mane
of willow trees, my mistress wind,
and pirouettes, perfumed by waves
over the summer's lilac skin.

The fluttering of purple eyes,
flows tonight beyond
the grassy sways, and lights upon
my captured breath in gusts again.

The aura of her cloudy voice,
embowered in the atmosphere,
whispers across the shifting stars,
and I'm compelled to chase her there.

Snow in April

She comes gliding down
the silver-latticed range
backlit by clouds,
and through the spruce trees
her body swirls and spins
faster, curls and spins faster,
her long, frosty gown unfurling,
grazing the stumpy legs
of her dance partners,
her wispy, pale arms
twirling from branch to branch,
the hollow echo of windsongs
calling the invisible steps
of this, her last wintry dance,
a promenade in white
before the warmth of spring.

Comfort of Clouds

On her morning walk
my father's specter guides her
along the wet sidewalks
through November fog.

Once home, she makes hot chocolate
and sits to look out at the sparrows
dancing on lonely branches.

The raindrops streak
outside against the window, erratic,
like they are trying to find their way
back to the comfort of clouds.

My Grandmother's Hair

During the day she laced it into layers
of delicate lightnings and monochromes
(it took several hours, some would later say),
and tucked it from the world with bobby pins.

It slept above the white sheets of her neck,
feral, nocturnal, and silver gray. It waited.
Not even the prairie wind could stir
from slumber its kinetic tendrils.

On weekends when she would let it free,
it tumbled down to her toes in silver waves,
waves away from a decade on the sands,
and drowned the time along her hardwood floors.

The years have gone. Her porcelain ring box sits
atop my daughter's silver dresser drawers.
The bobby pins are stored inside. If I lean close
I feel that ocean crashing into shores.

Girl Unbound

She knew the legend of the waning heartbeat
and a voice that never answered.
Sparrows crossed the sky as fireflies
on those nights she went nocturnal.
Her heart jumped the layers of patchwork,
so strong the stitching ripped the distance to her veins.
She spent the remaining dark
sewing fabric to keep from wanting to be that light.

But the old stories were not true.
Even as the sparrows multiplied
she couldn't bind the beating down.
Those fireflies grew inside her.

One night her veins glowed through.
The sound of her own voice was more than fiction.
Along the darkened road the ground thumped.
Her pulse quickened.

The old folks looked up from their porches
and noticed the warming of her skin across the grass.

The Earth Exhales

At dusk, when the sun is liquid,
the world believes.
Trees hold up the clouds
with only the strength of their branches.
Light slips under this umbrella,
and in the moment hovering,
before the shadows swim like whales into our view,
you hear the earth exhale.

Out on the horizon, there's an ancient face,
invisible and staring back at us.
We feel the wind through our hair,
and we remember when.

The Echolocation of Owls

An owl calls through the spruce trees,
encrypting thoughts into the wind.
I try to tune to that frequency, tune
until the translation escapes white noise.

I lie back in the deep grass, let
my breath slow to the pace of clouds.
I stare into the dark branches,
notice the flow in those phantom waves.

Wherever I was going will have to wait
for these pictures in currents of sound.
I close my eyes and listen
to the shape of voices sliding over air.

This Prairie Shore

There's a sky in central Wyoming
where the world looks through
from the other side,
and in the looking,
finds a way back to itself.

Seashells hide inside those clouds.
Put your ear to the wind
and you'll hear oceans
breaking across the earth in circles.
The circles join us to each other.

If you were here with me
we'd walk the length of this prairie shore.
We'd leave our words behind
and stare out at the tides,
red and purple and billowing in return.

Somewhere on an ocean shore
lovers find different clouds
twisting and wrapping around themselves
like bodies of sagebrush.
The sea-salt wind carries a memory

of Wyoming and sweetgrass rain.
It's nearly evening or
it's nearly morning—impossible to tell.
The clouds are seas that connect us.
The wind, a circle to ourselves.

The Curator of Shipwrecks

It has taken him centuries to measure
the rain near the shores, and longer still
to learn how far the scrolling thunder scrolls.
He taught himself the ways
the waves eavesdrop on the murmuring tides.
He translates the whispers of undertows
and knows the lore of driftwood from shipwrecks
long ago wagered across the bed of the ocean floor.

When the broken flotsam breaks the sands
he's waiting, knee-high in water,
ready to decipher their circular patterns
like the weathered runes of ancient stones.
Their wooden stories like our own, interrupted
by distant calls foaming through the fog:
an incandescent song useless to ignore,
drawing us towards the cutlass rocks.

Watching Your River Sleep

Sheets turn to rivers.
We are the tangled shores.
We diverge the distance between us.
Pillows bank the fluency of your hair.
The half-light from the window
paints leaves on the walls as waterfalls.

There are archetypes I knew but never said.
The swells and undertows.
Where do those currents dream
they want to go?
I cannot rest. I would drown
myself to know.

The Search

We formed a search party that night
and gathered at the edge of the ocean.

The tidal winds spoke to our lanterns;
each candle slumbered in succession.

When the others stopped and wandered off,
I remained to look the length of the shore.

I noticed the moon alone
highlighting the sand and the footprints there,

outlines like my own, leading out sea,
broken by the rhythm of the waves.

Shorebirds

All night we wandered sands.
We saw the shorebirds in their rags.
They skirt the salty waves, the edges
that only together are possible.
They dipped their talons in white noise
along the rising foam.
Under a boomerang of tides
they flashed their silver feathers.

There we stumbled upon ourselves
in the owling of our hours.
The ocean intertwined.
Waves knew forever.
Our toes blended in swells.
The silver of our second skin
moved like a thing alive
just below the covering of sea.

Overflow

Everything is born
again at sea. When I
made love to her
I remembered
why, to slip my skin,
to shed my mind, to swallow
rivers of her hair.
The old story wasn't true.

Once it rained a year
or more, but never long
enough to flood
the known and unknown
worlds. We made love
in those waters.
Our arms were branches
floating on the sea.

Sea Creature

Our past was always ocean bound.
Lost in those watered lands,
it could only wash ashore undone.

Someday sitting on a beach of your own creation,
inhaling the salted air of your new lover,
you'll notice something flashing in the sand.

You'll wish for an empty, intact shell
so you can hear the ocean
unbound and crashing twice.

Instead, you'll find a shipwrecked thing
gasping in the concrete air,
its gills like weighted clouds.

You'll take the foaming creature
and throw it back to tides.
You'll leave the broken shell for someone else.

Out Walking After Storms

Rain holds dear its old lovers,
the footfalls and puddles
sunk in the old familiar steps
beyond memory
where light reflects like crayons in the blood.

Your shadows slip their chains
a second time drunk on skies.
They follow you home
to find you at your doorstep
kissing the wind, its tongue the taste of cinnamon.

In a world without color,
carrying a fire within,
watching the same and endless night,
when you make love
all you think is *halcyon*.

Tonight, below the passing cars,
I hear your stray voice like headwaters.
I remember giving you my jacket in the storm.
Darkness ran forever.
The rain whispered then fell asleep.

To the Tides What Follows Touch

Each day we throw ourselves into the shore.
We blend and go and swirl again
without the same shipwreck.
Evening brings the salted winds,
the taste of our skin in the shadows of the palms.
The weight of where we've come
between the grains of sand.

We leave to the tides what follows touch,
each footprint a splash of moonlight
pulling us past the undertows,
out to where the currents find their way.

The Drowning Years

Long before the water rose, I knew.
Billowing dark against the sky,
the end was a storm unbreakable.
Years earlier, that ghost began.
Our bodies touched like wind.
I'd put my ear to the grass
and hear those banshee calls
through the dark ocean of earth
from some future echolocation.
I couldn't mask those phantoms
even with the cloud breaks of fatherhood.

At night I dreamed the rain would seep
into earth like blood.
It fed whatever was coming.
I ran outside without my shoes.
The earth swelled below my feet,
the approaching flood,
enough to drown
ever more the both of us.

We Were People of the Dark

In the days before illumination
we only went by nightfall.
We ran like animals under a new moon
across the surface of ourselves.
During the day we followed clouds
and risked the shafts of light,
our heartbeats through our skin,
to find those caramel shadows.

Silence was a way through the crevices
as we crossed through the sagebrush of our love.
We knew the thoughts of deer
at dusk, why suddenly they appeared
at the edge of the highway,
ready to leap the headlight beams.
On the other side, alone,
the warm ocean of the dark.

Remembering

In the ocean of his fatherhood he went to drown
the man he used to be. Each morning he held
his memories under the water until they stopped
and sunk into the tides. Each night
he felt the creatures of prophecy swimming
against the undertows like salmon on a river run.
He did not tell his family that he'd gone
to meet the creatures in their tributary flows.

They found him later washed along the gravel beds
gasping liquid oxygen and flailing for the sea.
His slippery eyes stared up at them, their figures
distorted by the presence of the air.
With their talons and their slipstream paws
they spread his silver, scaly ashes everywhere.

Troll Crossing

There are uncertainties traversing our unknowns
despite the trolls we've ostracized under the bridge
of our relationships. These ogres contemplate
us from the abutments of our past: how and when
and where to snatch us by our limbs. At night when we
are drifting down to sleep we glimpse the glistening
of their red tethered eyes reflecting off the walls.
It's not the gentle cycle of our snores we feel
but their hot breaths in the pulsing of blinking lights.
On Sunday afternoons when the lazy sparrows of
our lives should linger on our beds, it's not the flutter
of wings echoing through the heavy air, but the gobbling
of feathers, the chewing of bones, the slow grind of dull teeth,
the grunts below our naked feet splintered by the crossing.

July

He crashes summer picnics,
the drunk uncle of June and August,
fire-tempered and boasting
that there will be no rain
as long as he's in town.

His breath smells of hot asphalt.
He sweats through his shirt.
Grass turns sallow
under his dry and dog-eared boots.
Best to let him drink
until he stumbles into fall.

Traveling Carnival Girl

She'll appear in the night,
her neon jewelry
blinking in rhyme.
She'll look at you
with her candy apple eyes
covered in caramel eyeshadow;
she'll whisper to you in the lyrics
of songs by Journey. *Don't stop
believing,* she'll say. *Hold on
to that feeling,* she'll say. She'll
pull you close and kiss you;
her perfume will smell
like buttered popcorn laced
with red licorice; her lips
will taste like funnel cake
sprinkled with cinnamon.
The sudden sugar rush
will tickle your brain, and you'll fall
into her carousel arms.
The last two things you'll see: her
cotton candy hair, her
rollercoaster curves.
The next morning, she'll be gone,
and all that will remain
in the dust of the fairgrounds
will be a pile of her bolts.

Making Love on Graph Paper

They touch
at the y-intercept
of the bed, their hands
rising over the run
of each other's shoulders,
the slope of their bodies
moving across the room
like algebraic squirrels
chasing each other through
a forest grid, hiding
under each leafy interval point,
and for an instant unseen,
conjuring things only unknown
variables could, things
only mathematics could describe,
equations we all
wish we had solved.

Separation

After our protracted war, I walk
wounded through the neighborhood.
I listen to the silhouettes of branches
winged against the sagebrush skies.
Those feathers want to sail untethered
in the air tonight. How they must imagine
currents to carry them drifting above
roofs of houses, away from all
their cold domestic views,
and free to scale
the world bound
by nothing more
than circumpolar
winds, they drop
near their lover's sea,
their roots happily loosed to sands.

Love Story

He spent his time collecting snow,
meticulously chasing the seasons
just to gather all the specimens
known throughout the world.

She listened to the dialogue of streams
and taught herself their foreign words.
Eventually the liquid codes
of riverbeds revealed themselves to her.

They met on the surface of
their melting waterways, his glance
reflected back to her the snowfalls
of her youth, the shrouds of frosted fog.

Her eyes were like blue fuses to the sea.
He imagined his future there
on shores where the wind reached the waves
stumbling like drunks into the sands.

They felt themselves fall through,
swimming in the water's spell,
the blending their tenses,
the fusion of their forms.

Flyscreens

Their love was a mobile
home where he wouldn't harm
a flyscreen. He preferred instead
the destruction of its walls.
For months he brawled
the demon echoes
of his past at their front porch
and tore away the siding
of her fragility. His fists
smelled like burning tin.

When all that remained
was the mesh of window screens,
she looked out at him
with her insect eyes.
He saw reflected back
a thousand times
the flaming tires
of his own pupils,
the place where he
spontaneously combusted
years ago.

Return

Trees lend shadows to the grass.
Sometimes that stray dog wanders home.

Sons looks for the fathers they never knew
in the middle of the forest.
They find the wind still reaches there.

One night, years later
she reaches across the ocean
of sheets to touch his skin.

On the edge of town,
a man holds a suitcase
full of sparrows.

He turns back to see
branches shaping clouds.

The Sacrifice of Leaves

The shrapnel of my father's toil
is embedded in my DNA,
and though my smokestack-chasing chromosomes
are woven in coils of industry,
I did not die in double shifts the way he did,
in machines that shatter drums,
in imploding mines that suffocate
the lungs. I've seen the winter's four am
reflected in his oil-field eyes, his stares
of drill-bit grinds. "Now go to college, son,"
my father said. "Don't be like this."
I never was and left his sagebrush town
a phantom of the working men who stayed.
Now at my desk, I breathe the purified
air of the middle class. I feel disguised
in thick neckties hanging me silently
among these modern courtiers whose fathers
worked with their window views. I am a feign,
but still the thing I learned to rage against,
lapping up the temple blood my father scorned,
and when I look at trees, all I see
are branches stripped, the sacrifice of leaves
to fall, how a tree's survival then depends
upon the darkened roots descending earth
for minerals, readying new
coming leaves for spring.

Searching Stars

He liked to skate his fingertips
across her palm at the table
when no one was watching them, liked
to tuck her hair, those strands of sunset,
behind her ear, to brush his leg against her leg,
the start of a slow-cloud dance. He leaned
to kiss the painted freckles on her cheek.

Later in the hotel room, naked, watching
her hips slide on top of him, he tried
to still the moment, touch her palms, her hair,
her legs, her cheek, but it wasn't enough
to learn her all, the freckles he wished he knew
like stars on the skies of her skin, the light
discovered over years and years of searching.

Albatross

Such distances are impossible to span
even with the length of wings.
Yet you, my albatross, you do it without fluttering.

You glide a hemisphere away
on the strings of circumpolar winds.
How could a flight go so weightless and alive?

That summer she was a continent from me,
I stayed grounded and listened
to the heaviness of rain.
I hoped she would let the wind anchor her.

I wondered if our dreams
were only instances of spring
slipping across the chasm of seasons.
There were so many things
to keep us grounded.
They all seemed made to carry.

If we had tried could we have gone unbound?

I think so.
I think so now.

Albatross, the years remain unchanged.
You still drift on the currents
of my whims. Your shadow fills my eyes.
You light upon these waters
without a thought of season
when the seafoam turns to snow.

Because you try.
Because you come unburdened.

Nowhere That Sagebrush Wants to Go

The highway is a gravity fenced by barbed wire.
Deer and antelope feel the pull of asphalt.
We know that same pull
beyond skies
where we'd go
if we could slip the fences
we create for ourselves.

The mountains in the distance
seem like pictures from a brochure.
We make ourselves believe
by running parallel.
We pretend we see the steel bumpers
coming from miles away
to meet us on the yellow line.

The deer jump. The antelope
press themselves to the ground
and cross smaller than they are.
Both feel their weight
nowhere that sagebrush wants to go,
Minutes later, their deaths, our deaths,
are glorious contortions.

Star Marrow

The gap between the stars is like memory.
We dream and the space closes.
We run the Milky Way
holding hands to reach the constellations.
Can we pull the stardust down
in a universe expanding at the speed of touch?
We cast our hopes into that space.
What comes back we eat raw.
The rest of our time we pick clean
the bones we find inside ourselves.
We break the marrow, the taste
of one another, enough to fill the distance.

Signals and Songs

I sing a nursery rhyme
to the shelter dog we've had for years,
playfully code the beats
on his gray-dusted snout.
His half-fold ears track the echoes
like antenna tuning to the frequencies
of signals across the time band,
invisible waves from prescient seas,
when girls sang of London bridges,
and younger dogs, so black and tan,
ran freely through the streets.

Our Dismal Science

The economics of your touch, a simple
concept, the quantity inversely tied
to price, so high, I cannot pay, the surplus
dusting away on shelves somewhere, the store
abandoned long ago in a part of town
I have not visited in years, and so
it goes, our time together sold like steel
or stereos or pasta shells in boxes
of cardboard, only pasta shells and steel
and stereos will fall in price eventually,
an equilibrium where sloping lines
of supply and demand cross in stasis
much like those times in our early days
when I would bring to you a spray of white
carnations filled with the smells of cinnamon,
so that the costs of roses appeared
as trivial as the moment (now looking back)
when you would take the flowers, and with
your free hand, rush your fingers through
my hair like we'd already bought the world.

Intuition

She ghosts her cursive on my back,
her fingers gliding the cotton earth
of my t-shirt, tracing the words
unknown but almost recognized.

They warm my skin to temperatures
of her inherent second sight.
Outside, familiar scents of firs
in new reunion with the snow.

Love Note

Along the highway
just above the cottonwoods

a flock of geese bend
across the blank page of sunset.

Their cursive wings
hover a moment in the salmon light.

You take my hand,
and with your fingers,

you trace our secret language
across the lifeline of my palm.

Outside the Museum of Nature and Science

We drove two hours from a land of sagebrush
to see, in Denver, a land of dinosaurs,
but all my son wants to do is run with water,
to guess with the children of strangers
where the fountain's spout will slip
to steal a ray of sun,
and in the stealing, pull laughter from the air.

There's something in unknowing
but knowing still, in the coming
but not coming of the water
that draws him there.
I feel it too, the gravity of the mountains on the skyline,
as if this water that jumps between the toes
comes from the snows of those rocky peaks,
water older than bones, the spray across our skin
that brings us human to ourselves.

Silver Muse

That night he wrote in charcoal verse
the cursive of her body's curves, her hips
gliding across the solitary page.
It was all that he could do
to form her out of snowflakes
rising in his chest. When he was through,
her hair fell in stanzas, her eyes
mirrored the softening of vowels,
the rhythm of her breath
metered so he could memorize
the moment there with her.
He wished she were his creator too,
the thin strokes of her fingers
smudging him into view, so they could bridge
the barrier and live inside the paper rhymes,
where their forms and silver words
would rise and intertwine.

How I Knew

In the corner room
when no one saw
you leaned down
and kissed my fingers.

I wanted the heat
of your phantom lips
pressed to my skin,
to burn that mark

for my future days,
so when I shook hands
with anyone
always they would see

the outlines of
those beautiful scars,
and wonder if echoes
felt cool to the touch.

Weightless

They were weightless travelers
across the earth untethered.
The story about their beginning
hidden in the grass but never gone.

Their voyage fueled by cirrus sky
took them over mountaintops,
then out above the sea.
They floated through twilight
into the mirrored atmosphere
until they edged to the edge of infinity,
where the moon became a song.

Holding hands, co-pilots,
they turned to each other,
their smiles like the echoes of a hundred miles.
Below them, earth.
Above, the stars.
In the middle, a universe like feathers.

The Divorce of Gravity

Her parents took a quarter of the moon.
She remembered them as thieves
when she was only seven.
They masked themselves with crescent smiles
and left her waning in the sky.
Each night she made up her own stories
out of the tapestries of constellations.
They were true in another galaxy.
The stars stayed clustered together
the same for centuries.

During the day, she was invisible.
Her parents kept their love somewhere
in another hemisphere.
She watched them turn the sun
on each other until they scarred.
How deep the burns, she never knew.
She only had those nights when she lit the world.
They looked back at her as satellites
unguarded in their gravity,
pulled toward each other in the dark.

Foreclosure

My father was sledgehammer
running into walls.
My mother, the sheet rock,
taped and textured and painted
to keep the insides of the house from showing.
They sparked the rock with alcohol.

From my room at two am, I heard,
hole by hole, the house come down.
Outside a monster made of string
circled through the neighborhood,
screaming the skies fell down.
Through the window I smelled
gas fields on its breath.

Plaster was a remedy for fools.
Everyone that came after
always felt and noticed still
the outline of those holes my father made.
Men like him, thousands,
leveraged into blunt objects, the women,
crumbled to foundations.

Water Cycle

My father kept his secrets under the surface of himself.
When he finally tore them out one morning
before the fog had cleared
he rowed to the center of a lake
somewhere west of town
and dumped the secrets overboard.

That's the story my mother told
a thousand times the same.
She left out the part about my father
ripping fragility from his veins
that same veiled morning.
He must have hoped to drain his way to seas.

We felt evaporation true,
the depths of the distance between them
from the wreckage and the silt
to the ripples on the surface of clouds.
On nights when it would thunderstorm
we'd let the raindrops melt into our tongues.

Hunchback

Teased for silence inside of silences,
he never raised his hand.
He slumped when walking under moonlight.
He noticed details others lost.

Roots grew under sidewalks and lifted the concrete.
Ants appeared
then disappeared in the cracks between the spaces.
It happened--the smallest of things.

While others talked and pointed,
he saw not only the intricacies
of interactions of the tiny,
more than roots and insects,

but those of people,
who carried with them a gravity
inescapable,
the beginning of a crack

smaller than sound,
unheard at midnight,
growing by the hour,
something only a bellringer hears.

It was the narrow beating of their hearts,
that sorrowful spider
crawling through their veins,
weaving a single thread.

Leaping from the Comfort of the Trees

When finally she felt the meaning of the world
she gathered up all the feathers
her ravens had scattered to the grass.
She held them in the sunlight.
What she saw, a midnight shadow
of her other self, the hidden one.
She wondered where those ravens dreamed to go
once they left the comfort of the trees.
She couldn't know, tethered there so long,
watching the smoke from her life
circle and fade into the air.

She waited for the solace of the wind,
when no one was watching, to make her leap.
The feathers were her veil, and more appeared
so the others from the trees could only see
her looking down and somewhat grounded.
Beyond those feathers, rising higher, rising strong,
that beautiful shadow stretched the distance to the sky.

A Love That Crosses Worlds

There's a love that crosses worlds
and pulls your light of blue
to shadows of my green.
In the fault-line snowflakes find a way.
They fall to us and melt our veins.
On the skin's surface
we come like clouds wrapped in wind.
Our subsurface is a candle
we follow in the dark.
It burns all through the night,
and in the morning
still we see it flickering.

Ticket to the Partial Earth

I stole a ticket to the partial earth with you.
We knew we could go anywhere,
but chose the frozen water.
Instinct was the sheet of ice
that hardened below our skin
and separated the flow of lights
from the lathered fog of air.

We lay face down, holding hands,
looking through the frosted window.
We stared into the dark below
waiting for something we'd never seen
to swim to the surface and find us.

At night, under the moonlight,
the window became a mirror.
We saw what we'd been looking for
but couldn't say in words,
our reflections staring back
like they'd finally found the world.

What Those Light Years Carry

Only the stars know what would have come.
They cast their prophecies
across millennia and leave their blooms of light
on the fingertips of branches.

We lie in the grass and we wonder
what those light years carry
through the heaviness of dark,
the friction of our choices
gathering stardust like a comet on its way.

Inside those beams it must be still,
the sound of the universe
falling like cotton rain against the window.
We could trace all those drops of accumulation
and watch them racing down the glass
in ways we never knew.

Ice and Bone

We are made of ice and bone
and the weight of our accumulation.
It holds us here like branches under snow.
Each day the snowflakes land on us
heavy from falling down.
We wait for the sun's alchemy
to melt us through to the other side
where we could see flush again.
It never comes, that forecasted magic
in our frozen world together.
Here resentment binds the wind
just for following horizons.

With a lion's mane we slumber.
With a lion's mane we winter on.

Hands That Were Our Own

This is the thing a father does.
He turns the summer range
into a summer wind.
He folds that wind into a map
which like a circle goes forever
into the atlas of your past.

We hunted arrowheads south of Buffalo
when you were nine and five.
Gleaming rocks in the prairie grass
were more than ideas of fashioned stone.
They were stories that could be true
in a world where men still heard the prairie songs.

We walked the day for a few broken points
chipped a thousand years before.
Those hands could have been our own.
I warned you of rattlesnakes warming in the sun.
You took turns keeping watch
and polishing the points with your fingers to make them real.

Near dusk we stopped at an outcropping to rest.
In the distance we heard coyotes howl
like they believed in the ghosts of men.
You asked me if they were wolves,
and watching how you held those arrowheads,
I told you that they were, and I believed.

The Space Between

This wind the mountains breathe
in Wyoming holds the memory
of everything the world has learned
before meaning went in search of words.
It ripples forward to the edge of town,
cherry in the sunset's glow,
the scent of wildflowers on its lips,
looking for the path of an old lover.

We meet this wave
and we remember too,
how once we wove the space between
the future and our reveries.
What continues in the dark
when no one listens,
the softer work of wolves,
the mountains and the vacillating sea.

Another Love Story

We navigate our waterways
without instruments.
We reach through a ceiling unattached to stars.
We blind ourselves willingly
to hear the old stories
of a bearded mariner
who clings to his driftwood
no matter the raging sea.
We save him from drowning
a hundred times or more.

We should know better.
His paper heart gets waterlogged.
The weight of his blood is too much
to carry. Once his veins
leak on the floor,
it's best to push him overboard
and leave him to the sharks.
They've been trailing in the water
as if they'll never leave
until they've torn something to pieces.

To the Woman Taking a Highway Sobriety Test

I judge you. I condemn you under my breath. I laugh
while you stumble
to walk a straight line, recite
the alphabet backward,
touch your finger
to your nose.

How deaf from alcohol you must have been
to drive the length
of this two lane highway where sagebrush is all we can believe.

Intoxication never imagined you,
your insect frame, your hair like elderberries.
Cars slow to pass the siren lights.
Your face is the color of the wind.

I think of the sorrow that caused your flight and the creatures
you thought you were leaving to find humanity out here
with sparrows weighting power lines.
They watch you stand and let your head back, your eyes
closed, your arms
outstretched until
the world spins
and crashes down.

To the Angry Guy at City Council Meetings

There was a time I could not understand
why you would suffer
through so many nights
alone in the front row of the room, as though
you sought a war,
your bloodshot eyes like pyres,
your fists like blinking lights, your neck
contorted in forced distress to keep you on
your self-created ledge of fury,
ready to pounce on each agenda item,
ready to lunge and yell, a sacrifice for all
the rest of us, our water rates, the cost
of firetrucks, landfill charges, and the rise
in the salaries of bureaucrats who think
they're smarter than guys like you.

But there are so many things,
so many transgressions
to keep the burning in your head that I
now understand why you require yourself
to write those letters to the editor
each week on topics like the height of weeds
or dogs that run wild in our streets.

There are
so many things,
that in a place like this it's easy to get drowned
in a lake of politics.

There are hunger pains
from wanting to matter to the world, the need
to stretch your arm, to raise your hand

so you can rise, so they can stop
and finally recognize
your voice from the others
blending into waves,
waves that never find
the silence of the shore.

Impossible the World

On the edge of our rescued shore
the snow sleeps in black and white.
It wants to dream simplicity.
Next to the water there's an empty bench.

The sun squints behind clouds,
enough to stare into our retinas.
It knows the truth before we blind,
but we blind ourselves anyway.

Once I took all the colors
I felt while kissing you
and released them to the wind.
I waited the night.
I listened for their sounds.
What came back was deeper,
impossible, the world.

The Chorus

In May the world renews itself.
You mistake those ghosts again
for your own resemblance.
Wildflowers in the hills smell like coming home.
Daylight hides the wind.
Leaves cover all the scars
of winter so you hardly remember
the way it was before.

Your own scars are like that,
secrets concealed by the season's end.
You and the birds forget the older songs,
how autumn sombers like an icy drum,
how we hurt each other suddenly
like the first winter storm
down from the mountain
to cover everything
in chorus after chorus
of that all-encompassing white.

A Way In

Sometimes our chariots are pulled
by hummingbirds. Their wings
flash little ghosts of silver
in the searchlight of the moon.

They create a ripple in the wind
the color of infinity.
It's the same ripple
we imagine passes through a lion's mane.

We swim through caverns to find a light.
That light is a ripple that never left.
We keep a pocket full of vines
for ripples tethered to the ground.

We let go of the handlebars
or remove them completely
before the ride begins.
We feel that tiny wind.

We close our eyes and run with cheetahs
to swell our veins again.
We climb into the tower and feel time
from the concussion of the bells.

We swim into the sea.
We listen to the whales
and their echolocation through water.
We return with knowledge of the tides.

A Way of Throwing

Throw your boomerang
into the quiet dark.
Aim unseen for everything
and hope for the unbroken,
some stardust, fireflies, or a lizard's skin
an hour before the dawn.
Hope for changing colors.

Don't force the boomerang into the light.
Your brain has a muscle memory. It gets in the way.
Your brain wants a rose garden.
Close your eyes and imagine a garden full of garden snakes.
They've returned to their instincts and intuition,
grown teeth to eat through shovels.
They don't care what's coming next.

You have your boomerang for finding out.
Throw it across the river and follow where it lands.
Then be sure to bring it back.

Once Upon a Time

Somewhere the world begins.
A book opens. A toddler stands.
The air smells like cinnamon.

A man lies in the branches of a cottonwood tree.
He notices the leaves flow like waves
just before they glide into the shore.

A seagull, thinking he's an albatross,
flies into the fist of circumpolar winds.

Spanish syllables let loose their hounds.
Soon you're running with the pack
gathering dandelions under the moonlight.

A poet swallows lava. The legend opens true.
His tongue forks lighting.
An old woman takes her last breath.

Her hand opens. A white carnation
blooms inside her palm.

Elegy

The wildflowers run their purple flags.
Fields are castaways.
The crescent moon is unattached again.
No stardust. No clouds.

You think you'll keep the memories of lovers
inside your pocket for easy travels,
but apparitions run
like mice across the snow.

You hear a woman's voice on the radio.
You reach. The airwaves have her gone
to another's ear a universe away.
The voice never called your name.

Coyotes howl because the silence is impossible.
The sparrows know a coyote's song
is a simple elegy to an empty sky
and the tonality of wings.

Long Dark Moon

One day you feel the light from a sunken place.
You'd missed it all the times before
on your way across the surface.
If you linger you can think its depths into existence.
No one notices but the world.
You lie in bed that night and watch shadows
turn into the future you hoped was true.
When you close your eyes
sleep comes like wind through trees,
and soon, those shadows slip inside your breath.

You dream the long dark moon runs naked through the sky
like an animal in the costume of a dreamer.
She drops to earth in an empty field.
Dirt softens between her toes.
Frost is her night gown.
She looks back at a sky without her form.
She smiles, then moves in the direction of your window.

Upon Julia's Laundry

Her red and purple blouses
are pinned topside down

to the clothesline
strung across the railing

of fire escapes stories above
the street and its murmuring.

They waver in the breeze,
their shadows billowing

through the apartment window
like the curves of a woman

shimmering as she walks away
in the warmth of the afternoon sun.

Strapless

The cottonwoods let down their leaves
in the heavy air of November.
Rain exfoliates their crusty skins.
Sparrows whisper rumors: the lucidity
of December, the hush of falling snow.
The wind yawns and exhales,
a breath rushing by and fading
in a burst of a season the next town over.
It been six months since I fell on black sky,
long enough for a reverse of weather.

Encore

The mason jar lives its afterlife
dressed as a blue vase on the windowsill,
but even in retirement old habits remain:
the preservation of carnations
clothed in formal white,
the scent of cinnamon rising from their lips.

Sleeping with Grizzlies

Our words are dead by midnight.
Each day we slip the silence
of our skin and run
to find the edges of those we want to love us.
It's too much for some, the weight
of vowels, the syllables
like a grizzly bear sleeping next to us in bed.
During the night, restless,
he rolls over and wounds us with his paw.
If we're lucky, it's the soft thunder that wakes him.
He sits up and asks to slow the clocks.
He tells us everything,
how lighting reflects the walls.
We hope the morning never comes.

The Atlas of Past Times

These maps of us I carry in my head.
Alone, I still trace all the old rivers
twisting through the liquid night.
They bring me floating back
to the headwaters where we began,
where we drank ourselves new.
There were no towns or cities to stop the roads
so we drove through
watching the land of open range
act out what happens.
We met so we could wander.
The sky was everything we touched,
the mountain range only inches away
but a hundred miles long.
The airwaves we never saw coming.
We couldn't name them or give them a latitude,
but they kept us going from page to page.

Blue

The light of the world was always blue.
It found a way into the colors that wonder,
the sheen in the black of a raven's wings,
the whispers of midnight snow.
There's the blue pull of the moon
that keeps young lovers in their gravity,
and once, when the wind was lost
it was winter blue that brought it back.

The second time I came to you
blue was the tremor in my veins.
Eventually your kiss returned those tremors
to the room spinning blue around me.
In those undefeated days
we walked out to the grass and rain.
Your eyes, the air, the smell of sagebrush, all of it
blue falling on worlds of blue.

Ahead Somewhere Between

There's a morning wind that feels us true,
me in my mountains and you on your plains.
The frequency is our memory.
A few minutes before the dawn
we remember the future
sleepwalks at the edge of the forest
if we'd only wake and run.
It's the same sleepwalker's fate that comes
when embers from a campfire die
and silence folds the universe
over us like a blanket.

Without a flashlight, we only have the stars
to guide us past midnight
when that wind swings a prophecy
like a lantern across the prairie grass.
We look for each other
ahead somewhere between.

Driving Across Wyoming

Sometimes the earth holds out its cherished things
for those who pay admission.
We watched from the highway
to see if those sunset myths were true.
Stretched across the shadows, the ancient light
held itself suspended above the mountains
and invited a path into ourselves.
We chased that glow to the horizon.
where it stayed warm for hours.
We stopped when the glow went out
somewhere near Crowheart
and saw the stars lift off their twilight veil.
Those lanterns swinging through the universe,
the wind over the prairie grass,
the world before the opening of views.

Undiscovered

When the world fell to the sea,
I measured then my life in silences.
I dissolved alone at night,
a snowflake in the water.
Ripples couldn't escape the sound
of the stories I told myself,
that we had once been the glistening
of foam across the rocks along the shore.

Wind brought those thousand lights
inland to all the little towns
where everyone was sleeping but couldn't sleep.
They rose from the quiet of their beds,
and through their windows they saw the night open
to the undiscovered stars.

The Secret Only Winter Keeps

On the path of a lion's mane
where do we find our way?
Like butterflies we present our own cocoons for showing,
the life and dance, a ballet of this curious world.

The steps are wild and tame together,
like the kiss of spring and fall,
the secret only winter keeps.

Our secret is that we walk in that snowfall
hidden by the fog and trees
searching for our own footprints and paws,

the life impossible,
the taste of magic upside-down
melted and dripping off our lips.

Day or Season of Throwing

We put a bottle in a message.
Inside the glass was everything we knew
captured in the depths of silica.
The smooth surface of our words
refracted what the world could see.

Neither one of us remembered
who threw the message into the waves,
nor the day or season of throwing.
It drifted through our middle years
in the currents of a sea we couldn't know.

One night lying in bed together
staring into the dark, both of us muted,
we felt the message near a distant shoreline.
Whether washed onto the sands
or shattered in pieces against the rocks,
we preferred the words broken
and buried on the ocean floor.

Cyclothymia

I feel I know the ways of water,
that it can hold the sky
even in a camouflage of clouds.
On the hillside the next town over
the billowing comes again.
I ignore it into existence.
It's far too heavy for the lighter air.

I lie awake at night and the ceiling stares at me.
From those heavy miles I feel a pulling of the world,
the syncopation of my skin.
I thirst for liquid stars.
If they were streams I'd drink
from the headwaters of those lights.
I would flow and never drown.

And I would glow and leave the empty dark.

Boom Town

Decades later the practice field
disintegrates. Antelope
take batting practice
against the wind's biting curveball.
Nothing escapes sagebrush
creeping across the diamond,
suffocating the pitcher's mound,
crawling over shredded chain link.

Before uranium had a heart attack
sleeping in its bed, the rusted bleachers were filled
with mining families,
and the men, all members
of the Lion's Club, stood
in the background, in crabgrass,
swapping familiar stories
of past wars and perpetual defiance.

Exodus

These kids are simply tumbleweeds.
Born by wind,
they roll across the prairie grass,
across the sagebrush,
through these Wyoming towns,
Medicine Bow,
Rock River,
Laramie,
and all the others,
on to the state border,
only stopping if,
by chance,
they're caught
in a snow fence
or the grill of a passing truck
on some highway
where the dust
never quite settles
and the wind keeps wailing,
wailing for its young.

Wyoming, The Last Chapter

They'll come, not as locusts or phantom
horsemen. Not as dragons or pits
of fire. They'll come as hordes,
carrying treasure from their conquered lands.

These gluttonous antagonists,
these thirty-five acre creatures.
They desire ranches cut to chunks.
They split generations. They eat
empty taxes and the comic book west,
where the natives whoop from the hillsides,
calling down thunder before battle,
where cowboys never miss,
riding bareback, their pop-gun rifles
echoing across the serrated plains.

Box Scores

Each morning the deities and lesser gods
spoon cornflakes into their flawless mouths.
They drink perfect cups of the purest coffee
before leafing through the newspaper.

Our lives are tucked away on page ten
in the middle of the sports section
and reduced to a series of box scores
smaller than horoscopes and weather forecasts.

Last week, you went one-for-five.
Is the cold front expected to last?
What's in store for Taurus next month?
They ask the questions that matter.

Barking into Silence

The rule is clear: you let a sleeping dog
lie, and that's fine in principle as far
as sleeping goes. It is the lying that
remains; the questions go unanswered still:
just how, or where, or when, or where again?
These questions matter in a world of rules
where, say, a thousand German Shepherds might
decide to sleep inside a subway station
or armies of Pomeranians
could pile at the gates of airport terminals
on command: barking into silence, silence
into the slumber of the friend of man
if we're not sure, if we don't take the time
to mind the interrogatives of our lives
as though they stood for our imperatives.

Reaffirming He-Man, Action Figure

You could have said something back then to me.
Perhaps when I was nine, that would have been
the time to tell me how a normal man
can't take a punch the way you've done and rise
again for more, that right hooks come (the left
hooks too) in life so fast like flurries wrapped
in fists of ice. And why not tell me then
that bad guys win--sometimes the worst--out here
without the chance for sequels? When you dangled
from cliffs, and destinies of humankind
depended on your nerve, you hardened your gaze
and turned the darkest moment into play
with help from me, your god from the machine,
who still believes despite the evidence
that I have sway, that I can intervene.

Once He Minded His P's and Q's

he perceived the world unpredictably:
it now quaked with meaning. The qualities
of words queried his perceptions.
On any perfectly random afternoon
he felt his pulse quicken. He found
a sudden, subtle pleasure in the pace
of a woman's voice, the quiet
resonance, perhaps at a quantum level,
in the purity of raindrops
queuing on the rooftops overhead,
the packs of commas quelled
by brief periods of consonance.

It wasn't long before he noticed
the power of the sounds were a rarity
together on the verbal clothesline
of vowels and consonants.
They caused peaks to quail, aquifers
to dissipate, and people to quit
the very place they'd occupied
so long, and pulled away by quatrains
of tempests inscribed with
the poetry of plosives,
they became, each one of them, a poem
quivering in the phonetic wind.

Staff Meeting

You turn your head for a moment.
A circus bear comes cycling in.
He bunny hops the table, juggles
bottles with his paws.
The tutu is just for show.
Soon the room is raining shards
of glass, but everyone stays mesmerized.
Storms and gyrations carry more the time.

You hear performance monkeys
clapping in the other room.
Someone added them to the agenda
without telling you again.
Back before you were anyone's boss
you only worried of simple carnivals,
the bearded lady, never really any trouble
once you listened to the feathers in her voice.

The World Imagines Rain

When I begin with you
I want to mention rain,
taste like rain coming
down in watered air.
If the weight that forms our lives
could be something the world
imagines, it would be the face
reflected in scarves of rain,
eyes wet with future.
We walk that maze forbidden,
the scarves invisible
brushing against our lips,
our breath like small clouds
billowing and billowing.

The History of Rain

The rain is a heavy lullaby
singing me to sleep from the open window
where all I see is a moonless blue.

I try to imagine a future in that song,
the swishing of the trees,
the soft thunder humming far away.

There's a history behind this rain
that doesn't have to be the truth.
If we talked tonight, we could tell the story
together the way we wanted it to go
so it pulled the space halfway for both of us.

How would it go, our rain song then?
The smooth voice of water in the dark,
a chorale ocean on our skin.

The Mariner's Guide to Sagebrush

Mariner of asphalt, you're tied again
to your mast out here on the high desert.
Wind follows the waves of silver grey
to the end of the sunk horizon.

Where there's life it tries to wander
from the heading you chose so long ago.
It wants to feel the slow crash of mountains
or the cool taproots of rivers.

All night the rain comes like seduction.
The smell of camphor, the sparrow's songs--
they pull at your traveler's bindings.
You want to drive into this giant hollow
and shelter with the grouse.

Above, an eagle cries.
You feel a loosening
like a herd of antelope
racing across the opening of steppes.

Elk Mountain, Wyoming

She sits on her prairie balcony
all the days of her infinite life
wrapped in a sheath of clouds,
her pine-cone hair sloping white shoulders.

She stares out at the horizon,
waiting for her southern lover
to cross the ocean sage
before winter casts its chains again.

From the seaside interstate,
you can hear his message boomerang
in a heavy wind, that's he's coming,
that he always was eventually.

The words harbor near her still.
She waits, her flintknapped pulse
in the rhythms of invisible waves
breaking over the tops of snow fences.

To My Son on His 18th Birthday

My growing pilot son,
today I wonder how I made your wings.
Because I am a mentalist,
instead of the builder my father was,
my illusions of the ground
are of little use to you
in a time of flying.

I hope my instructions are intuitive.
Fly to heights you must believe,
beyond a world the skies put on.
If you have to fly beside the sun
where tongues fork lightning,
then find a way through fire and rain.

When you were born I knew this day
would come, when you would need
more than a man's thick regret.
When the nurses looked away
I dipped your tiny wings
in my thunderstorming veins
so you would never stop
to think of falling from those clouds.

Hiking the Snowy Range with Treyjan, Age 12

We didn't climb because we could,
we climbed to escape the ground
that arose and eroded between us.

Granite shouldered thin our weight
atop that alchemy of earth
where hawks rode their thermal winds.

The silhouettes of their feathers
spread across our view
and kept us sheltered from the midday sun.

I was still your tether then,
though I was the tethered one.
You leaned back and yawned.

We stayed for hours,
letting those wing beats brush across our skin.
I hoped the night would never come.

Seaside Wyoming

There's another reason for the wind.
It brings us news from the Pacific Ocean.

It travels twelve hundred miles,
the taste of sea-salt on its lips,
to whisper dreams of seashells.

Those whispers are the way of lovers
from the memory of distant shores,

longing for mountains,
the pine air clean like sagebrush rain,
the open glow of salmon skies.

Less of What Remains

Just as snow rides the mountain down
to drive the streets in white,
so too can a man can lose himself
in half meanings. He packs a suitcase
with regrets and promises.
He walks in the direction of his youth,
always due north,
where the sagebrush grows as big as men
and storms pick clean what's left.

In the spring runoff a hiker finds the bones
or less of what remains in a ravine.
The flesh has gone to streams.
Near the body lies the suitcase,
where something kicks from inside,
nudging the suitcase forward,
trying to continue.

Escaping Our Sagebrush Town

We bulldozed through the coffee stains in streets
and waited for the dusk to cover us.
We searched for ways to rise above our veins
filled with the oily blood of our fathers' past,
the DNA of a roughneck's full regrets.
We knotted the shoes of pop machines and pulled.
They fell. We watched as they ached and belched
their twelve ounce cans. We gathered the trove
in bags in hopes of trading it for beer,
then drove away and laughed our pirate laughs,
our thoughts of transcending that lonely place
surrounded by a sagebrush moat we knew
too well. We finished at the ledge of town
and listened to the wind screaming to get out.

The Morning You Were Born

Somewhere between the moon and Mercury
the clouds said something of your name.
Without sleep my body hollowed.
My fuel was the light of dawn
and the thought of your arrival.

I drove through the streets on fumes
of how far the world could now travel.
Traffic signals blinked their silent string.
The flowers of cherry trees
glowed red with electricity.

On the AM radio, a woman sang.
Her voice wandered
across the frequencies
from what seemed like ten thousand miles away.

Constellations

The wish a fallen star makes upon itself
contains a whisper.
If you could hear the words,
they would include a valley in Wyoming,
just below the Tetons, a secret buried,
a lock to solitude.
There, a girl could reach the constellations
if she wanted to find a way to herself
without wishing the future true.
Meaning could live in a milky way.

All night the stars kept running
like a comet's tail through the atmosphere.
They found her stardust,
holding hands with her windy lover,
looking up and looking back
in time. And there, a key
lying in the grass.

Tetons

Rocky whales
with cloud-tipped fins

dive sideways down
into a jagged sea,

swallowing the pine trees
like tiny plankton.

Bison mariners
float in the distance,

riding the crests
of prairie waves.

Vertigo of Clouds

There comes a vertigo remembering
the ways we were like clouds,
tracing the edges of ourselves inside.
Born on a lantern wind
we disappeared and circled back again.
Everything we discovered there
came down in rains of buried light.
Invisible but visible,
without the touch of knowing why,
our suspicion falling to the horizon.
The sky left a blue field that doubled forever
as we huddled and leaned into the night.

Half Song, Half Thunder

I mean to change myself again,
but the silent letters of my name
I've omitted and released to the night.
Where they've gone
and where they're hiding in the world
seems impossible without a guide
and the navigating stars.
To search for those words, I stare into the clouds.
They change like a wheel of clover,
but all the feinting lights, they never stop spinning
in this delicate machine.
The silence, severed from its life,
hides behind and tastes like rain.
It wants to come back, however long.

I close my eyes, refute nothing,
tune myself towards another's quiet.
I listen. The wind through trees
is half song, half thunder.
I find my way in the waters of that song.
I can get those letters back.

Gypsies in the Night

When there was nothing else to burn
I found my motives moving with the fog.
I embraced it with my reasons.
I ignored the story about digging two graves.
Instead, I dug a solitary one
as deep as a witch would know.
Inside that grave I buried everything,
the pang of ice, colors in the shape of fire,
and the wraith that crawled
through the synapses of my head.

I knew never to return again,
to let the fixed stars govern
how the world should be.
Whatever emerged from the wet earth
would wander like a gypsy in the night,
and I would be somewhere far away.

The Origin of Ghosts

Without the void,
there would be nothing
on the other side of leaving.

Inside the dark
matter between us, a sorrow,
the phantom's journey
of a million empty stars.

Beetle Kill

Here, the lodgepole pine
die with silent dignity:
knights succumbing
to a war of attrition
after decades holding this range;
now too long weathered bronze
by a dark, six-legged sun,
and bludgeoned a thousand times,
they bleed a fungus-blue
from their hollow ribs
and watch it dry
down their crusted toes.

Too exhausted to fight,
they remove their green chain-mail,
letting the needles drop,
and face the winter exposed.
Should they survive the cold,
these stoics will surely burn
in the dry-ice heat of summer,
and no doubt,
they'll leave their last words
to someone else.

The Lineage of Stars

So many poems have come before, it gets
a little overwhelming. Pardon then
this poem for its timidity. Forgive
me, its creator, for considering
the fate of my tiny fire (or so I think
it burns) in galaxies of poems that hurtle
across the universe at phantom speeds
towards the other galaxies of poems,
billions of them, sometimes exploding in
a supernova pyre, light-years away.
Still, to burn near burning bests no fire at all.
I dip my finger in these stardust streams
and trace my fragile poem still glowing hot
among the lineage of all these stars.

Intimacy

Towards the dusk when I was tired
from walking home, I heard the river
whispering its synonyms
in the voice of polished stones.
I wandered through the grass
to the crescent of the shore.
My feet sank in the sidewinder flows.
The burdens on my narrow veins
were washed away downstream.

Upstream something moved in the ripples of citrus.
I knew it swam my way.
Inside, I felt the silent stir
of freshwater arrhythmias.
There was nothing to do but wait
to see what nakedness emerged.

My Heart the Youngest Animal

I watch this empire sun
extend its last remaining light
across the range of sagebrush
like a hand that can't let go.
I understand the reasons why.

Nothing but mountains in the distance.
Along the highway, no cars
shimmering like dots on the horizon.
Maybe there's no one
for at least a hundred miles.

Whatever made this world
also made the rising and falling of my breath
slow like the movement of old ghosts.
And then my heart, the youngest animal,
wanders off to chase the afterglow.

Let Your Light Guide Light and Further Light

Because you have these lights
like fireflies inside, because
you have the unencumbered night,
the choices are release or guide them free
where they desire in time to wander.

The years and decades can find a way
without them, the deathbeds too, the glow
gone dark to the silent forests of men.

It's in this dark you must stay and stand
and let your light guide light and further light,
and by seeing the secrets of hidden dark,
emerge only in that silence.

Chaperon the lanterns that follow,
their lights huddled and waiting
to take you farther still.

Live Like Wind

To live you must learn to live
your life like wind.
You chose this place for a reason.
That reason doesn't have to make sense.
That reason
doesn't have to settle
like sunset light.
It can simply fall beautiful to you.

Search for the empty spaces,
the long path home.
Come like wind atop the waves across the farthest sea.
Meaning gusts forward
without a song.

To live you must live like wind.

About the Author

Aden Thomas (also known by his real name, Thomas Johnson) grew up on the high plains of central Wyoming. He has worked as a dishwasher, laborer, retail manager, educator, community developer, and public agency executive. He has a bachelor's degree in English Literature from the University of Wyoming. His poems have been published over a hundred times in various literary journals and small magazines over the world. He lives near Laramie, Wyoming. He hopes you visit him at his website:

www.adenthomas.com. Or email him at adenthomas@gmail.com.

Made in the USA
San Bernardino, CA
26 November 2017